The Choice Is Yours

Introduction

Whether you're already a teen or on the road to becoming one, you're in a very tough but important part of life. It's easy to get lost in the struggle with so many ups and downs and big choices you've got to make every day. Maybe you're having a hard time getting along with your parents, making friends, getting good grades, or dealing with peer pressure.

Most of the time, you can't control everything around you. But here's the good news: you can control yourself and make good choices. With every decision in life, the choice is always yours. It's never too late to change, and there's always room to improve.

SCHOOL
FRIENDS
DATING
WORK
DRUGS

CROSSROADS OF LIFE

To **Help**
You **Deal...**

...with real life, we are giving you a set of tools called *The 7 Habits of Highly Effective Teens*® — seven characteristics that happy teens all over the world have in common.

The 7 Habits of Highly Effective Teens®

HABIT **(1)** **BE PROACTIVE®**
Take responsibility for your life.

HABIT **(2)** **BEGIN WITH THE END IN MIND®**
Define your mission and goals in life.

HABIT **(3)** **PUT FIRST THINGS FIRST®**
Prioritize and do the most
important things first.

HABIT **(4)** **THINK WIN-WIN®**
Have an everyone-can-win attitude.

HABIT **(5)** **SEEK FIRST TO UNDERSTAND,
THEN TO BE UNDERSTOOD®**
Listen to people sincerely.

HABIT **(6)** **SYNERGIZE®**
Work together to achieve more.

HABIT **(7)** **SHARPEN THE SAW®**
Renew yourself regularly.

Getting the **Most** out of This **Activity Guide**

So what are you supposed to do with this activity guide, and what is it supposed to do for you?

The 7 Habits of Highly Effective Teens will help you achieve your goals and build great relationships with everyone you meet. Give these activities a chance, and they can make a big difference in your life.

Here are a few suggestions for getting the most out of this experience:

1. **MARK UP THIS BOOK!**
   Take out your pencils, pens, or markers to highlight what you like and to take notes.

2. **BE CREATIVE.**
   Create meaningful pictures if you feel like drawing instead of writing.

3. **APPLY WHAT YOU LEARN.**
   Focus on improving yourself by practicing what you've learned at home and at school.

WELL, I GUESS IT'S TIME TO RENEW MYSELF.

To Learn More

The 7 Habits of Highly Effective Teens, by Sean Covey, has sold over 3 million copies and has helped teens all over the world! If you want to learn more about any of these activities, check out the book or visit these websites:

www.seancovey.com/teens

Get in the Habit

ACTIVITY I

Habits

Habits are things we do repeatedly, but most of the time we're hardly aware of them. Try folding your arms across your chest three times in a row. You probably did it the same way every time. Now fold your arms again, but switch the arm that you place on top. Feels weird, doesn't it? Our habits are what put us in autopilot mode most of the time.

The Good, the Bad, and the Ugly

Brainstorm all of your habits below. It doesn't matter if they're good habits or bad habits; just list them.

Example: I make my bed every morning.

....

....

....

....

....

....

....

© FranklinCovey. All right reserved, including the right of reproduction in whole or part in any form.

Principles

A big part of having a successful life is to live by good principles. Have you ever heard of the law of gravity? You know, the law of nature that says if you fall off your bike, you're going to hit the ground... hard. Like the law of gravity, principles such as honesty, respect, hard work, and love never change; they never let you down. All of the principles we live by make up our character.

Who Do You Admire?

Think of the people you admire, such as parents, teachers, friends, or even a book or movie character. What do you admire about them? Think about their character and the principles they live by.

PERSON	PRINCIPLES
Example: Daysa	*She always works hard.*

To learn more about principles, read pages 24–26 in the Teens *book.*

6 – Get in the Habit

Paradigms

Another word for perception is paradigm (pronounced pair-a-dime). A paradigm is the way you see something or your point of view. We all see the world in different ways. The way we see the world affects the way we look at ourselves and others. For example, if you believe you can't make friends, you'll do things to support your belief. Or if you believe you're smart, that belief will change what you do in class.

The keys to a great life are to choose to live by good principles, to learn to change your paradigms from time to time, and to develop good habits that will get you to where you want to go.

OH WOW! PARADIGM SHIFT!

Paradigms, Principles, and Habits

Use the Word Bank to solve the crossword puzzle below.

ACROSS:

1. The way we see the world, others, and ourselves.
5. Never change and build character.
6. Feeling affection for others.
7. Always telling the truth.
8. Things we do repeatedly or automatically.

DOWN:

2. When others can count on you.
3. Sticking to something until it's finished.
4. Helping others in need.

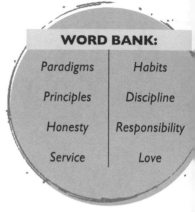

WORD BANK:

Paradigms	Habits
Principles	Discipline
Honesty	Responsibility
Service	Love

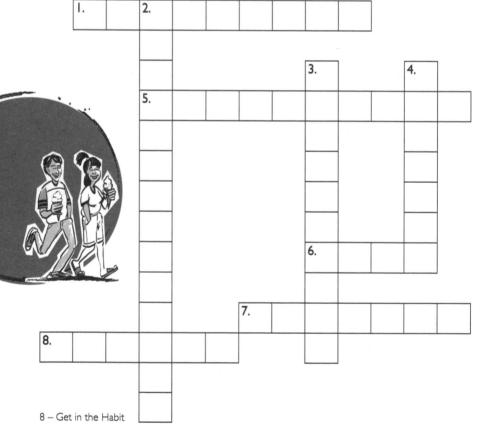

8 – Get in the Habit

TRACY, I THINK YOU NEED A NEW **CENTER**!

The Right Stuff

An important part of a successful life is centering it around the right stuff. Often we center our lives on possessions or on other people, but friends change, relationships end, and things wear out. When you've centered your life on something unstable, you'll find that your life is unstable as well.

To discover what your life is centered on, just ask yourself what you spend most of your time thinking about. The answer might surprise you.

The Center of Your Life

What do you spend most of your time thinking about? Do you stress over anything (for example, clothes, boyfriend/girlfriend, popularity, friends, parents, school)? Brainstorm your ideas below.

Example: Getting good grades.

....

....

....

Why do you think you center your life on these things?

Example: I'm afraid I won't be able to go to college if I don't get good grades.

....

....

....

To learn more about what you should and shouldn't center your life around, read pages 19–23 in the Teens *book.*

Get in the Habit – 9

It's as Easy as...

Rightnow, you're probably thinking that habits are a big deal, so they must be really hard. Actually, developing any habit you want is easy! You can developahabitbypracticing it for 21 days.

Create New Habits

List some of life's biggest challenges right now. Maybe you're having a hard time turning your homework in on time, or maybe you want to make more friends.

Then think of some new habits you could have to help you with your challenges. List them next to each challenge or draw your new habits on page 11.

CHALLENGES	NEW HABITS
Example: Homework	*I will turn in every assignment on time.*

HOW I WILL DEVELOP THESE HABITS

Example: I will finish my homework before I watch TV.

DRAW YOUR CHALLENGES AND NEW HABITS HERE.

Don't forget to **PRACTICE** your new habits for **21 DAYS!**

HABIT

Be Proactive

Choose How to Respond

How do you react when someone cuts in front of you in line? Do you yell at him, or just let it go? If you get in a argument with your best friend, do you tell her off and avoid her for months, or do you forgive her? About 100 times a day, we get to choose how we respond to different situations.

How Would You React?

Write how you would handle each of the following situations.

1. While you and your little brother are home alone, he makes a mess and then blames it on you.

....

....

2. While taking a test, you look at the person across from you, and he or she is looking at your paper.

....

....

....

3. As you're walking down the hall, you overhear a bunch of your friends talking about you behind your back.

....

....

....

A Lesson from Soda Pop

What if one of your friends gave you a can of soda pop that he had been shaking for the last 5 minutes? Would you want to open the can?

Reactive behavior is just like a can of soda pop that explodes when the pressure builds. Proactive behavior means thinking before you act and being cool and calm.

Proactive and Reactive Behavior

What other things does reactive and proactive behavior remind you of?

Draw or write them below.

REACTIVE BEHAVIOR IS LIKE . . .

Example: A volcano

PROACTIVE BEHAVIOR IS LIKE . . .

Example: A bottle of water

Proactive and Reactive Language

How can you recognize reactive and proactive behavior? **All you have to do is listen to the way someone talks. Here's how reactive people talk:**

"That's me. That's just the way I am." What they're really saying is, *I'm not responsible for the way I act, and I can't change.*

"Thanks a lot. You just ruined my day." What they're really saying is, *I'm not in control of my own moods; you are.*

Notice how reactive language takes the blame away from the speaker and places it on someone else?

Proactive behavior is always in control. Proactive people say things like, *I choose to . . ., There's gotta be a way,* and *I can do better than that.*

Say What?

The chart below is full of reactive statements. Next to each reactive statement, write a corresponding proactive statement.

PROACTIVE LANGUAGE	REACTIVE LANGUAGE
Example: I'll do it.	*I'll try.*
	That's just the way I am.
	There's nothing I can do.
	I have to.
	I can't.

For more examples of reactive language, read page 51 in the Teens *book.*

16 – Habit 1: Be Proactive

A Can-Do Attitude

A can-do attitude is very important for getting you to where you want to go in life. Can-do means that you make things happen; you don't wait around for something to happen to you. If you want to make the basketball team, you practice every day. If you want to have more friends, you find ways to meet new people.

Remember, can-do is not pushy and annoying. Can-do people are persistent and motivated. They know what they want out of life, and they work hard to get it.

The Sky Is the Limit

If you want to make a sports team or get good grades, you need a can-do attitude. Use the space below to draw a picture or write about some of the things you want to accomplish this year.

....

....

....

....

....

NOTHING CAN HURT "PROACTIVE MAN"!

Flex Your Proactive Muscles!

Have you ever thought about what makes superheroes so—well, *super*? They take control of a situation, flex their super-sized muscles, and help others.

Once you've learned to be proactive instead of reactive, and once you become a can-do person, you're on your way to becoming a superhero (without the costume and x-ray vision, of course).

Have a Proactive Day

Start flexing your proactive muscles today. In the space below, write different ways that you can start being more proactive.

I WILL BE PROACTIVE TODAY BY . . .

Example: Using proactive language when I talk to my family members.

....

....

....

....

....

....

HABIT

2 Begin With the End in Mind

When I Grow Up

Have you ever thought about what you want to be when you grow up? Even though you have a long time to choose what you want to do with your life, it's important to start thinking about it now so you can make the right choices along the way.

Discovering your interests and strengths is a big part of deciding what you will do with your life. When you understand what your passions are and what you're good at, you will have a better idea of what you might want to do when you grow up.

The Great Discovery

Answer the following questions to discover your interests and strengths.

Describe a time when you were deeply inspired.

....

....

....

....

....

....

....

If you could spend one day in a great library studying anything you wanted, what would you study?

....

....

....

....

....

....

To learn more about beginning with the end in mind, read page 73 in the Teens *book.*

Who Are You?

Have you ever taken the time to sit down and think about what you're good at and what you're passionate about?

The Local Informant

Family & friends declare: "Gr-r-eat guy!"

Take Some "ME" Time

Answer the following questions about your

Five years from now, your local paper does a story about you, and they want to interview three people: a parent, a brother or sister, and a friend. What would you want them to say about you?

....

....

....

Think of something that represents you—a rose, a song, an animal. Why does it represent you?

....

....

....

If you could spend an hour with any person who ever lived, who would that be? Why that person? What would you ask?

....

....

....

E=MC²

Picture This...

Imagine you've just been given a jigsaw puzzle without a picture on the front of the box. How do you put it together if you don't know what it's supposed to look like?

Habit 2: Begin With the End in Mind is about living your life with a picture in your mind of how you want it to turn out. You don't have to decide every detail of your life right now. Beginning with the end in mind is simply thinking beyond today. Decide the general direction for your life so your daily actions will eventually get you to where you want to go.

Word Match

Match the words on the left with their definitions on the right.

BLUEPRINT	*Directions for baking a cake*
OUTLINE	*Instructions for building a house*
RECIPE	*Structure for writing a paper*

Why do you think beginning with the end in mind is important?

....

....

....

Mission Statements

One of the best ways to create an end in mind is to write a Personal Mission Statement™, which is like a personal motto that explains what your life is all about. For example, Nike's motto is *Just Do It.*

Personal mission statements come in all shapes and sizes. They can be a couple of words long or a poem or song. When you write your mission statement, express what is most important to you and the way you want to live your life.

Your Personal Mission Statement

To get started on your mission statement, write your name in the middle of the web diagram. Then come up with some positive words that describe you.

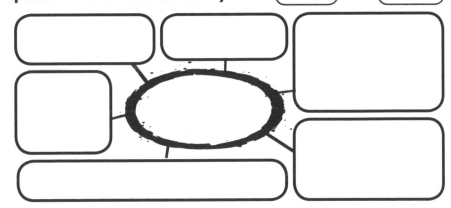

loyal

funny

Ahmad

courageous

hard-working

Now use the space below to begin writing your mission statement.

....

....

....

For more examples of mission statements, read pages 81–83 in the Teens *book.*
Habit 2: Begin With the End in Mind – 23

Who Do You Want to Become?

Life is short. The decisions you make today willhaveabig-timeimpact on the life you live and the person you become. Youareyoungrightnowandyourfuturehasn'tbeendetermined yet, so why not create a really great life for yourself and make a big difference in the world? You can start today!

(speech bubble: HEY, LOOK WHAT I FOUND. IT'S ME!)

Thinking Ahead

Imaginethatyou'vetraveledintothefuture. Whatkindofperson do you want to be a year from now?

Example: By next year, I want to be nicer to my friends and more optimistic.

....

....

....

....

What kind of person do you want to be 5 years from now?

....

....

....

....

HABIT

3 Put First Things First

There's So **Much to Do!**

Do you ever feel like there's not enough time in the day to do everything you want to do? Maybe you feel you never get to do the things you really want to. Or maybe you nevergetaroundtodoingthe things that really need to be done.

Add the Hours

Okay, it's time to do some addition, but it won't be hard. Next to each activity on the following page, write how much timeyouthinkittakesyoutocompleteit. Ignore activities that don't apply to you.

When you're finished, add up all the time you spend every day doing everything you need to. The results may surprise you.

ACTIVITY	TIME
Sleeping	
Getting Ready for School	
Eating	
Classes	
Homework	
TV	
Free Time	
Family	
Friends	
Internet	
Other	
TOTAL TIME	

To learn more about Habit 3, read page 105 in the Teens book.

26 – Habit 3: Put First Things First

The Key to Success

ACTIVITY 2

It can be difficult to do important things, like resisting peer pressure or overcoming your fears. Successful people are willing to make sacrifices from time to time and to do things they don't like doing because they know these things will help them achieve their goals.

You Can Do It!

What things would you like to accomplish that require a lot of hard work, discipline, and sacrifice?

Write what you want to achieve in the middle of the web diagrams on the next page, and then write several ways you can accomplish it. Don't forget to include things you will have to sacrifice (like some TV time) to reach your goals.

Ask for extra credit assignments.

Get Straight A's

Study harder for tests.

Do homework before watching TV.

What I Want to Accomplish

ACTIVITY 3

Big Rocks and Little Rocks

Putting first things first means planning your time around the most important things in your life—your big rocks—and then getting to everything else—your little rocks.

Sometimes living Habit 3 isn't so easy when you choose to study while all your friends are at the mall or watching TV, but fortunately there's a big payoff for people who choose to discipline themselves and do the important things first.

What's Most Important to You?

Think about the big rocks and the little rocks in your life right now. Think about what is extremely important to you. Then think about the things you spend time doing that could probably wait.

Draw a square around your big rocks, a circle around your little rocks, and an X over any activities that just aren't important to you.

HOMEWORK	READING	EXERCISE/FITNESS
SLEEP	GRADES	VIDEO GAMES
SPORTS	FRIENDS	MOVIES
SURFING THE INTERNET	MUSIC	SHOPPING
RELIGION	TELEVISION	BOYFRIEND/GIRLFRIEND
	FAMILY	

To learn more about big rocks and little rocks, read page 113 in the Teens book.

Habit 3: Put First Things First — 29

Make a Plan

Now that you know what your big rocks and little rocks are, you should plan every week around them. When you plan, sit down and think about what you want to get done in the week ahead. Set aside time for your big rocks first. Then schedule all your little rocks.

Why is planning so important? Because once you waste time, you can never get it back. Planning helps you accomplish more and live up to your potential.

Plan Every Week

List all of your big rocks this week. Maybe you have a big test to study for, or you need some extra sleep.

Then schedule time for all of your big rocks.

BIG ROCKS:

....

....

....

Monday	Tuesday
Wednesday	**Thursday**
Friday	**Saturday**

Overcome Your Fears

Fear whispers, "You can't do it," or, "They may not like you." If you listen to your fears, you'll miss out on a big part of life. To put first things first, you'll have to stretch yourself and leave your comfort zone. The comfort zone is what you're familiar with, and it doesn't take guts to stick with what you're familiar with. Learn to identify your fears and plan ways to overcome them—this is the courage zone.

Making new friends, standing up for your values, and speaking in public belong in the courage zone. In this zone, you'll find adventure and risk as well as growth and opportunity. Living in the courage zone is hard, but it's the only place where you will reach your full potential.

They Aren't That Scary After All

List your biggest fears below. Concentrate on the fears that keep you from doing your best and enjoying life, like talking to new people or speaking in public.

Then on the next page, write the worst and best things that could happen to you if you faced it.

MY FEARS

Example: I'm afraid I'm not good enough to make the basketball team

1.

2.

3.

4.

THE WORST THING THAT COULD HAPPEN TO ME

Example: Try out for the team and get cut.

1.

2.

3.

4.

THE BEST THING THAT COULD HAPPEN TO ME

*Example: Try out for the basketball team and make it. Play the game I love.
Be a part of the team.*

1.

2.

3.

4.

"*Acting in the face of fear*"

For more tips on overcoming your fears, read pages 117–121 in the Teens book.

The Relationship Bank Account

ACTIVITY I

Your Relationships

Take a second to think about all the relationships in your life. Brothers, sisters, mothers, fathers, good friends, bad friends, aunts, uncles, coaches, teachers, grandparents—all of these people are part of our lives, whether we like it or not.

A Relationship Check-Up

How are your relationships right now? Are they healthy or unhealthy? Fill out the chart below so you can see which of your relationships could use a little work.

HOW ARE YOUR RELATIONSHIPS?	LOUSY ←→ EXCELLENT				
Friends?	1	2	3	4	5
Siblings?	1	2	3	4	5
Parents or guardian?	1	2	3	4	5
Girlfriend or boyfriend?	1	2	3	4	5
Teachers?	1	2	3	4	5

Now pick any relationship in your life and write about it below. Is it good or bad? What makes it a good relationship or a bad relationship?

....

....

....

To learn more about the Relationship Bank Account, read page 131 in the Teens book.

What Does Relationship Mean?

Relationship is a big word. It's also an important word. A relationship is the connection you have with someone. The people we come in contact with are a big part of our lives.

Imagine that everything you owned was taken away from you. What would you be left with? Probably your family and friends—that's how important relationships are.

Relationship Reminders

What do relationships mean to you? Maybe there's a scene in a movie that makes you think about your family. Maybe a song reminds you of your friends. Think about the following categories, and then write something that reminds you of a relationship.

Example: Song: "We Are Family," by Sister Sledge

SONG

....

....

....

MOVIE

....

....

....

QUOTE OR POEM

....

....

....

MEMORY

....

....

....

WORD

....

....

....

SOMETHING ELSE

....

....

....

The Relationship Bank Account – 35

The Relationship Bank Account

The Relationship Bank Account is like a checking account at a bank. You can make deposits and improve your relationships, or you can make withdrawals and hurt them. Keeping promises, doing small acts of kindness, and apologizing are deposits. Gossiping, breaking promises, and being selfish are withdrawals. Every good relationship you have is the result of making a lot of deposits over time.

One Deposit at a Time

Decide whether each coin below would be a deposit or withdrawal. Then draw an arrow from each coin to the appropriate piggy bank.

Compliments · Smile · A Kind Note · Apologize · Insults · Stand Up for Someone · Ignore · Keep Promises · DEPOSITS · Break Promises · Hugs · Listen · Hold a Grudge · Keep to Yourself · WITHDRAWLS

Small Acts of Kindness

Have you ever had one of those days when nothing seems to go right? Then suddenly someone says something nice to you that turns your day around?

The Golden Rule says to treat others as you want them to treat you—that's what small acts of kindness are all about. They are the little things that can make big differences in other peoples' lives.

Relationship Cash

What small acts of kindness will you do? Fill out the coins below with all the little things you can do to improve your relationships.

Be sure to think about all your relationships: your family, friends, teachers, coaches, etc.

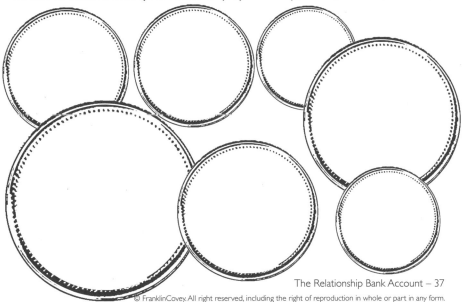

The Difference You Can Make

Choose to start building great relationshipstodaywitheveryone you know. You'll be surprised at the difference you can make in somebody else's life by making regular deposits. If you have damaged relationships in your life, fix them. It may take awhile, but stick with it. You'll be a lot happier and a lot more successful if you do!

Make a Difference This Week

Choose any relationship in your life—a family member, a friend, a teacher, a coach.

Write how you can make a positive difference in this person's life this week.

....

....

....

....

....

....

....

4 Think Win-Win

ACTIVITY 1

Common Attitudes

I'M BETTER THAN YOU!

TOTEM POLE

WELL I'M BETTER THAN HER!

AT LEAST I'M BETTER THAN YOU.

I'M A LOSER!

Think Win-Win is an attitude that says I can win and so can you. It's not me or you; it's both of us. Relationships aren't competitions. We're all in this together, so we might as well look at each other as equals and develop a win-win attitude. Here are some common attitudes that keep us from thinking win-win:

WIN-LOSE: This attitude says, "I don't care how good I am as long as I'm better than you."

LOSE-WIN: This attitude is weak. It means you get stepped on because you're the "nice guy" and give in all the time.

LOSE-LOSE: This attitude says, "If I'm going down, then you're going down with me."

Identify Your Common Attitudes

Take the following quiz to see if you have any of these common attitudes. Be honest with yourself. Circle your choice.

ATTITUDE	NEVER ←——→ ALWAYS				
I get jealous when my friends win.	1	2	3	4	5
I usually end up last.	1	2	3	4	5
I look for weaknesses in others.	1	2	3	4	5
When I fail, I hope others fail too.	1	2	3	4	5
I always want to win no matter what.	1	2	3	4	5
I'm not good enough at most things.	1	2	3	4	5
I always try to be better than others.	1	2	3	4	5
If I'm not good at something, I don't like others to be either.	1	2	3	4	5
I get angry in sports or competition.	1	2	3	4	5

For more information on these attitudes, read pages 146–153 in the Teens book.
To learn more about Habit 4, read page 145 in the Teens book.

How Everyone Can Win

A 13-year-old girl named Natalie was invited to sing the National Anthem for an NBA playoff game in 2003. In front of a televised audience, Natalie began to sing and then stopped. The 20,000 spectators fell silent as Natalie forgot the words.

Natalie hid her face behind the microphone, humiliated and unable to continue. But what happened next would inspire everyone who watched that night. Mo Cheeks, the head coach of the Portland Trail Blazers, approached Natalie and put his arm around her. Smiling, he turned her head once again to the crowd and started singing where she had left off. Soon Natalie joined in, and then the entire arena began singing the National Anthem along with them.

Even though the Dallas Mavericks eventually beat the Trail Blazers, everyone in the stadium won the night that Natalie sang the National Anthem. They learned that competing wasn't as important as bringing everyone together to help Natalie finish the song.

Help Others Win

Can you think of a time when you did something to help a friend succeed? What did you do, and how did it make you feel?

....

....

....

A Win-Win Attitude

Win-win is a belief that there's plenty of success for all of us— not just you or me, but everyone. You can have a win-win attitude by believing that we are all equal, and that nobody is better than anyone else. Below is a great example of a win-win attitude. You probably think this way more often than you realize.

You want to go to a movie. Your friend wants to go to dinner. Together you decide to go to a movie and pick up food to eat at home afterwards.

It's okay to want to win when you're pushing yourself to succeed —like in sports—but when it comes to relationships, everyone should win.

Win-Win Scenarios

Circle the numbers of the situations below that are good examples of a win-win attitude.

1. Skyler gets elected to the student counsel and works hard to treat everyone equally.

2. Carlee gets upset because Scott (the boy she's got a big-time crush on) asks out her best friend, Abby. Carlee starts spreading rumors about Abby.

3. Alex and Cayden both try out for the football team. Cayden makes the team, but Alex doesn't. Even though Alex feels terrible about not making the team, he is genuinely happy for Cayden.

4. Kelsee wants to go to the mall, but Maggie can't because she has to study for a math test. Instead of going to the mall alone, Kelsee helps Maggie study and they both go to the mall later.

5. LaTeisha and James are working together on a science project, but they both have different ideas. Instead of listening to LaTeisha's ideas, James completes the science project for both of them using his idea.

Why are these good or bad examples of win-win attitudes?

....

....

....

....

....

....

....

For more examples of a win-win attitude, read pages 152–154 in the Teens *book.*

Habit 4: Think Win-Win – 43

How to Think Win-Win

So how do you do it? How do you learn to practice Habit 4? It all starts with you. If you are confident and don't depend on others for the way you feel about yourself, you'll start enjoying other people instead of feeling threatened by them.

LET'S FIND A WIN-WIN SOLUTION, DAD.

Win the Private Victory

You need to be confident in yourself and realize your talents before you can be happy for others. Take a couple of minutes to write or draw some things that make you unique.

SOME OF THE THINGS I'M GOOD AT

Example: I'm good at math.

The **Advantages** of a **Win-Win Attitude**

Thinkingwin-winiscontagious. Peoplewithawin-winattitude are magnets for friends. If you help other people succeed and recognize their success, friends will be drawn to you.

Plus, a win-win attitude is useful in so many situations, from working outproblemswithfriendstoimproving your relationship with your family members. Thinkingwin-winalsomakes you feel good. It fills you with positive feelings and gives you confidence.

Create a Win-Win Attitude

List several different ways that having a win-win attitude can improve your relationship with the following people.

Example: I can ask my teacher for extra credit assignments to help my grade.

PARENT OR GUARDIAN

....

....

....

TEACHERS

....

....

....

FRIENDS

....

....

BROTHER

....

....

SISTER

....

....

COACH

....

....

BOYFRIEND/GIRLFRIEND

....

....

....

For more advantages of a win-win attitude, read pages 159–161 in the Teens *book.*

46 – Habit 4: Think Win-Win

HABIT 5

Seek First to Understand, Then to Be Understood

ACTIVITY 1

Listening Styles

Listening is a skill that is just as important as reading, writing, or speaking, but a lot of people don't take the time to become good listeners. Just like a baseball player who hasn't learned to swing a bat properly, some people have poor listening styles like these:

- **SPACING OUT:** Letting our minds wander when someone is talking.

- **PRETEND LISTENING:** When we aren't paying attention but pretend we are by using words like "yeah," "cool," and "okay."

- **SELECTIVE LISTENING:** Paying attention only to the part of the conversation that interests us.

- **SELF-CENTERED LISTENING:** When we see everything from our own point of view instead of standing in someone else's shoes. We say things like, "I know exactly how you feel."

Do these listening styles sound familiar?

Turn to the next page for a listening experiment!

A Listening Experiment

Turn to a partner and ask him or her to tell you about something that happened last week.

While your partner is talking, practice "spacing out" or "pretend listening." See if he or she can guess which style you are using. After 1 minute, switch roles.

Have you ever had conversations like these before? How did it make you feel?

....

....

....

....

....

To learn more about Habit 5, read page 163 in the Teens book.

Listen with Your Eyes

Every single person in the world needs to be understood. If you want to have great relationships with other people, take time to really listen to them and try to understand what they're saying. If you do, people will open up to you, and you will make tons of new friends.

An important part of being a good listener is learning to listen with your eyes. This idea might sound crazy at first, but noticing what people are trying to say with their facial expressions and body language is just as important as the words they are speaking.

Emotional Charades

Find a partner and practice listening with your eyes.

Take turns expressing as many of the emotions below as you can without using words. Then see if you can guess which emotions your partner is showing.

IMPATIENT	STRESSED	
ANGRY	EMBARRASSED	TIRED
SCARED	FLATTERED	FRUSTRATED
CONCERNED	SAD	HAPPY
RELAXED	EXCITED	THINKING
INTERESTED	NERVOUS	BORED
DISINTERESTED	CONFUSED	SURPRISED
WORRIED	ANNOYED	

Real Listening

MIRRORING PHRASES

"I can see that you're feeling . . ."

"So what you're saying is that . . ."

"You feel that . . ."

Real listening is about *mirroring* what someone else is saying. Why mirrors? Well, mirrors don't judge or give advice; they reflect. Mirroring is repeating back in your own words what the other person is saying and feeling.

Mirroring phrases help you understand what someone else is really trying to say.

Mirror, Mirror

Turn to a partner and pick one of the situations below. One person should be the speaker and the other person the listener.

HELLO! HELLO...

The listener should use mirroring phrases to try to understand the speaker.

SITUATION 1: Anna just failed her math quiz. She is scared that she might have to retake the class, which would make her fall behind her friends in school.

SITUATION 2: Alex is stressed out because he doesn't have enough money to go to the movies with his friends. He wants to borrow some money from his family members, but he's afraid of what they will say.

HELLO!

SITUATION 3: Abbie just broke up with her boyfriend, and she's upset. They had to break up because he lives too far away.

To learn more about genuine listening, read pages 171–176 in the Teens *book.*

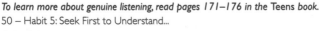

ACTIVITY 4
Communicating
With Your Family

Communicating with your family is really
important. Have you ever considered that maybe
you don't understand your family as well as you think you do?

**Two amazing things will happen if you take time to understand
and listen to your family members. First, you'll gain a greater
respect for them; and second, you'll get your way much more
often. It's true! If your family members feel you respect and
understand them, they'll try to understand and respect you as
well.**

Get to Know Others

**Understanding other people is a lot easier when you have taken
the time to get to know them.**

Turn to a partner and ask him or her some questions from the list below to find
out two things you didn't know about him or her. If you don't like any of these
questions, feel free to add your own.

Favorite subject in school?

Summer plans?

Favorite music group?

Favorite movie?

Famous person they'd like to trade places with?

Favorite celebrity crush?

Dream job?

Favorite sport?

Favorite food?

Take Time to Listen

There's a saying that goes, "People don't care how much you know until they know how much you care." Think about a situation when someone didn't take the time to listen or understand you. Were you open to what he or she had to say?

You can show how much you care by simply taking time to listen without judging or giving advice.

Be a Better Listener

Think of an important relationship in your life. Write some ways you can improve it by becoming a better listener.

....

....

....

....

....

....

....

....

....

HABIT

HONK!...

HONK

6 Synergize

Let's Get Together

What does *synergize* mean? Synergy happens when two or more people work together to create something better than either could alone. It's not your way or my way but a better way, a higher way.

HONK

Discover Differences

People who synergize see differences as strengths, not weaknesses. Everyone you meet is different, but have you taken the time to appreciate the differences?

Think about people you know who match the descriptions below. Write their names in the boxes below. Use the blank boxes to come up with some other differences that aren't listed.

Speaks another language		*Good cook*
	Good athlete	
Likes to study sciences		*Plays a musical instrument*
Writes stories, plays, or poetry		*From a different country*
	Good artist	

To learn more about synergy, read page 182 in the **Teens** *book.*

Habit 6: Synergize – 53

ACTIVITY 2

Working
Together

Once you've learned that differences make everyone stronger, you are ready to synergize.

How Many Ideas Can You Come Up With?

Turn to your partner. Come up with as many uses for a cup as you can. Be as creative as possible. Remember, the sky's the limit!

USES FOR A CUP

Examples: 1. It can hold your pencils.
2. Put it on your head and use it as a hat.

Teamwork

Many people believe the 1992 U.S. Olympic basketball team was the greatest sports team of all time. With players like Michael Jordan, Magic Johnson, and Larry Bird, the team beat its opponents by an average of 44 points a game. The whole team played so well together that, since 1992, basketball has become incredibly popular all over the world. That team became known as the Dream Team, and they won the gold medal because they synergized.

Synergy is about coming together to create something better than anyone could have done alone. If you've ever played sports, participated in a really fun group project, or played in a band, you've felt synergy. It's exciting to work with other people to create something amazing, and it also helps build relationships.

Your Dream Team

Imagine that you have been given the responsibility of putting together a team to create a new invention. You have a month to create your invention and then present it in front of an audience.

Who would you choose to be on your team? Why would you choose them?

PERSON	REASON
Example: Marcel	He always keeps his cool under pressure.
1.	
2.	
3.	
4.	
5.	

To learn more about teamwork, read pages 200–210 in the Teens *book.*

Habit 6: Synergize – 55

Getting to
Synergy

Whetheryou'rearguingwithyourparentsorplanningaschool activity, you can *get to synergy.* Follow this simple process.

Getting to Synergy
Action Plan

1. DEFINE THE PROBLEM OR OPPORTUNITY
Alfonso wants to go to a movie on Friday, and he invites Josh. Josh says that he would really like to go, but he is swamped with homework. His parents won't let him leave until it's all done.

2. THEIR WAY Seek first to understand the ideas of others.
Really listen and try to see their point of view.

3. MY WAY Seek to be understood by sharing your ideas.
Try to help them understand your ideas.

4. BRAINSTORM Create new options and ideas.
Get creative. Just shout out your wildest ideas, but don't criticize the ideas of others.

5. HIGH WAY Find the best solution.
After brainstorming for awhile, the best idea will usually go on like a light bulb over your head.

Ifyoufollowthisprocess,amazingthingswillhappen.Butgetting to synergy takes a lot of maturity because you have to be willing to listen to other people's ideas.

To learn more about the Synergy Action Plan, read pages 195–200 in the Teens book.

Practice the Plan

Turn to a partner and read the problem listed under #1 on the previous page. One person be Josh and the other person be the parent.

Use the Synergy Action Plan with your partner to solve Josh's problem.

Celebrate Differences

No difference is better than another; they are all just . . . well, different.

Celebrators see differences and diversity as advantages. They've learned that two people who think differently can achieve a lot more than two people who think alike. Celebrating diversity means encouraging and appreciating differences no matter what they are.

What Makes You Different?

A big part of synergy is knowing what makes you different and how you can contribute to a group.

List some things that make you different.

Example: I am really good at skateboarding.

....

....

....

....

....

HABIT 7

Sharpen the Saw

AAHHH... "SHARPEN THE SAW" IS MY FAVORITE HABIT...

ACTIVITY 1

Keep Yourself Sharp

Pretend you are walking through the woods when you see a man trying to cut down a tree with a saw. He's sweating and looks exhausted, so you ask him how long he's been working.

"About 4 hours," he says. "But I'm not really making any progress." Then you notice that his saw is completely dull.

"Why don't you take a break and sharpen your saw?" you ask.

Habit 7: Sharpen the Saw is about keeping yourself sharp so that you can better deal with life. It means paying attention to the following four dimensions of your life.

The Four Dimensions of Life

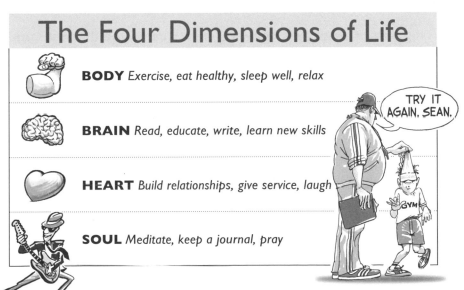

BODY *Exercise, eat healthy, sleep well, relax*

BRAIN *Read, educate, write, learn new skills*

HEART *Build relationships, give service, laugh*

SOUL *Meditate, keep a journal, pray*

TRY IT AGAIN, SEAN.

Take Care of Your Body

During your teen years, you'll have to decide how you'll take care of your body. Will you use it or abuse it? Will you fill it with junk food? Will you take the time to exercise? The choice is yours, but taking care of your body now will give you a huge advantage later in life.

Brainstorm different ways you take care of your body now and some things you need to change to take better care of it.

HOW I TAKE CARE OF MY BODY NOW	THINGS I NEED TO CHANGE
I play basketball with my friends after school.	I will cut down on all the junk food I eat.

For more tips on caring for your body, read pages 208–209 in the Teens book.

THAT SOCRATES SURE HAS A WAY WITH KIDS!

Take Care of Your Brain

Choose today to have an educated mind. An education means much more than good grades or a diploma hanging on a wall. It's a tool you can use to create, analyze, imagine, and dream. You have tons of ways you can improve your mind—like traveling, learning to play a musical instrument, listening to the news, reading, and writing.

Brain Food

How are you going to "feed" your brain? Write down a few things you want to learn. Maybe you want to travel, learn another language, or play a musical instrument.

SOME THINGS I WANT TO LEARN

To learn more about caring for your brain, read pages 216–224 in the Teens _book._

Take Care of Your Heart

Taking care of your heart is about making deposits in your Relationship Bank Accounts. You should also make daily deposits in your Personal Bank Account as well. This account works just like your Relationship Bank Account, but each deposit is just for you. You might laugh, sing, build lasting friendships, and pass along small acts of kindness.

Joke Around

Make sure you take time to laugh every day. Children laugh a lot more than adults do, and children always seem a lot happier than adults. Laughing relaxes us and makes us healthier.

Write about something funny that happened to you. It can be your favorite joke or a memory that still cracks you up.

Example: I made Katalina laugh so hard in the cafeteria that she blew milk out of her nose. Then I started laughing so hard that I blew milk out of MY nose!

....

....

....

....

....

....

For more ways to take care of your heart, read pages 228–233 in the Teens book.

Take Care of Your Soul

The soul is what's hiding deep down inside you underneath everything else. It is where you find peace and inspiration.

Taking care of your soul is very important. More important than what goes into your body is what goes into your soul. You can "feed" your soul by meditating, listening to music, serving others, writing in your journal, reading inspiring books, drawing, praying, or thinking deeply.

Soul Food

We all have certain songs, books, and movies that inspire us and "feed" our souls. What are some of the songs, books, and movies that make you want to be a better person?

BOOKS

Example: Where the Red Fern Grows, *by Wilson Rawls*

....

....

....

SONGS

Example: "You Raise Me Up," by Josh Groban

....

....

....

MOVIES

Example: The Lord of the Rings, *based on the books by J.R.R. Tolkien*

....

....

....

For more tips on caring for your soul, read pages 234–240 in the Teens *book.*

Make It Happen

Do you think you don't have time to sharpen your saw? With school, activities, studying, sports, and chores, you might be struggling to just get enough sleep. But choosing to take 15 to 30 minutes a day to sharpen the saw will help you today and in the future.

You're probably spending more time sharpening the saw than you realize. Homework sharpens your mind. Athletics help you care for your body. Making new friends "feeds" your heart, and listening to your favorite music inspires your soul.

Find Saw-Sharpening Time

Turn to a partner. Brainstorm several things each of you will do this week to take care of your body, mind, heart, and soul. Write them below.

BODY	MIND

HEART	SOUL

A Personality Exercise

The following exercise isn't meant to tell you everything about your personality, but it's a fun look at some of your characteristics and personality traits. It was taken from *It's All in Your Mind,* by Kathleen Butler.

Read each row and place a 4 in the blank next to the word that best describes you. Then place a 3 in the blank for the second word that best describes you. Do the same for the final words using a 2 and a 1. Repeat the process for each row.

Example

Imaginative	2	Investigative	4	Realistic	1	Analytical	3

COLUMN 1		COLUMN 2		COLUMN 3		COLUMN 4	
Imaginative		Investigative		Realistic		Analytical	
Adaptable		Inquisitive		Organized		Critical	
Relating		Creating		Getting to the Point		Debating	
Personal		Adventurous		Practical		Academic	
Flexible		Inventive		Precise		Systematic	
Sharing		Independent		Orderly		Sensible	
Cooperative		Competitive		Perfectionist		Logical	
Sensitive		Risk-Taking		Hard-Working		Intellectual	
People-Person		Problem Solver		Planner		Reader	
Associate		Originate		Memorize		Think Through	
Spontaneous		Changer		Wants Direction		Judger	
Communicating		Discovering		Cautious		Reasoning	
Caring		Challenging		Practicing		Examining	
Feeling		Experimenting		Doing		Thinking	

Now add up your totals (don't include the example, of course) for each column and place the total in the blanks below.

COLUMN 1	COLUMN 2	COLUMN 3	COLUMN 4
_____	_____	_____	_____
Grapes	**Oranges**	**Bananas**	**Melons**

If your highest score was in column 1, consider yourself a grape.

If your highest score was in column 2, consider yourself an orange.

If your highest score was in column 3, consider yourself a banana.

If your highest score was in column 4, consider yourself a melon.

Now find your fruit below and review what this may mean to you.

Grapes

Natural abilities include:	**Grapes may have trouble:**
• Being reflective. • Being sensitive. • Being flexible. • Being creative. • Having a preference for working in groups.	• Giving exact answers. • Focusing on one thing at a time. • Organizing.
Grapes learn best when they:	**To expand their style, Grapes need to:**
• Can work and share with others. • Balance work with play. • Can communicate. • Are noncompetitive.	• Pay more attention to details. • Not rush into things. • Be less emotional when. making some decisions.

Oranges

Natural abilities include:	Oranges may have trouble:
• Experimenting.	• Meeting time limits.
• Being independent.	• Following a lecture.
• Being curious.	• Having few options.
• Creating different approaches.	
• Creating change.	

Oranges learn best when they:	To expand their style, Oranges need to:
• Can use trial and error.	• Delegate responsibility.
• Produce real products.	• Be more accepting of others' ideas.
• Can compete.	• Learn to prioritize.
• Are self-directed.	

Bananas

Natural abilities include:	Bananas may have trouble:
• Planning.	• Understanding feelings.
• Fact-finding.	• Dealing with opposition.
• Organizing.	• Answering "what if" questions.
• Following directions.	

Bananaslearnbestwhenthey:	To expand their style, Bananas need to:
• Have an orderly environment.	• Express their own feelings more.
• Have specific outcomes.	• Get explanations of others' views.
• Can trust others to do their part.	• Be less rigid.
• Have predictable situations.	

Melons

Natural abilities include:	Melons may have trouble:
• Debating points of view. • Finding solutions. • Analyzing ideas. • Determining value or importance.	• Working in groups. • Being criticized. • Convincing others diplomatically.
Melons learn best when they:	**To expand their style, Melons need to:**
• Have access to resources. • Can work independently. • Are respected for intellectual ability. • Follow traditional methods.	• Accept imperfection. • Consider all alternatives. • Consider others' feelings.

"You can't make footprints in the sands of time by sitting on your butt. And who wants to leave buttprints in the sands of time?"

—Bob Moawad